THE WIDOW'S MITE & MIGHT

Written by Kristin Gerlach

Illustrated by Oliver Chen

BLANK PAGE

One day Jesus was walking through a busy town with the people he loved.
He looked toward the temple and saw the rich putting their gifts into the treasury.

One put 2 bags of gold and the other 10 bags of silver.
Everyone stared in wonder and envy.

Jesus saw also a poor widow putting in a single mite.
No one else noticed.

Jesus said, "Truly I say to you that this poor widow has put in more than all."
Everyone was shocked and confused.

He said, "all these out of their abundance have put in offerings to God, but she out of her poverty put in all the livelihood that she had."

"He sets the lonely in families," the widow nodded to Jesus,
leaving her burden behind and taking with her a prayer.
At that the rich people ran away from Jesus, but the children ran to him.

Then the children came to Jesus and said,
"We have no money to offer, what can we give?"

Jesus loved them and smiled, "Little ones, you can give the thirsty a drink. Feed the hungry."

He said, "you can clothe the naked and visit the sick."

"You can visit the imprisoned and and welcome the foreigner." Jesus said.

Jesus hugged them and went on his way. For Jesus knows his children understood.

THE END.

DEDICATION.

This storybook is dedicated to my son.

ABOUT US.

Shop author Kristin Gerlach's library of
Christian children's illustrated storybooks on www.amazon.com

Also enjoy Kristin's colorful storybook
Sauce of The Spirit: *How Grandpa Grills up the Tasty Fruits of the Spirit.*

BLANK PAGE

For where your treasure
is, there your heart will
be also. ~ Matthew 6:21